The Splinter
and
the Lamp

ሥንጥር እና ጉሎ

Collections of Poems

2026

Author's earlier works:

Author- Shiferaw Desta

Publisher- ZeGeray Desta

- **Fragmented Dreams"** (*Shirfirafi Hilmoch*) and
- **"The Ink and the Parchment** (*Dequana ena Qelem*)

A Key to the Threshold

In the opening pages of most books, one often meets
a section titled "Introduction." In my view, the
primary role of such a page is to provide a "bird's-
eye view" of the work.

However, while an introduction points to the
entrance, it rarely ensures the reader's journey
through to the end. To bridge this gap, I have
adopted an architectural metaphor: for one to truly
enter a building, they must not only pass through
the door but also navigate its entire structure. When
a building is completed and prepared for service, its
name and purpose are clearly displayed at the
entrance for all to see. Thus, every person who
enters does so with a foundational understanding of
the space they are about to inhabit.

Following this logic, I wish to provide you with a
"Key to the Threshold"core concepts to hold in your
mind as you navigate this collection. With these
insights as your guide, I invite you to journey with
me from the first page to the last.

"Sintir and Gulo" (A Splinter and a Lamp) is a
collection of over one hundred short poems. This
volume marks my third published work, following
my earlier collections, **"Fragmented Dreams"**

(*Shirfirafi Hilmoch*) and **"The Ink and the Parchment"** (*Dequana ena Qelem*). There are, however, distinct qualities that set this work apart from its predecessors.

For instance, to narrate history, share fables, and deepen the reader's comprehension, I have deliberately woven rich metaphors throughout these poems. Metaphor is the "salt" of language; it seasons our interpretation and sharpens the reader's insight. This is a universal truth, essential not only to Amharic but to all languages.

As the pen of an aspiring poet, I have looked to reflect my personal worldview—my own inherent philosophy—on social and human-centric issues. I must emphasize that these reflections stand for a personal strategic point rather than a collective consensus. Distinctively, I have introduced vocabulary that may feel distant to urban society but stays the heartbeat of daily life in rural Ethiopia. My aim is to introduce urbanites and non-Amharic speakers to the authentic flavor and rhythm of the countryside without losing its original essence.

This is a testament to the **authenticity and originality** of the work. To help the reader, I have provided footnotes for these terms at the bottom of the relevant pages. Furthermore, to introduce Amharic poetry to a global audience, the poems are presented in a bilingual format. I wish you a meaningful journey through these pages.

Contents

1 The Enduring Provision 13

2 The Path of the Unwary 14

3 An unanchored heart 15

5 Tether and Parchment 17

6. The Softening Grace 18

7. No Smoke Without Fire. 19

8. The Toll of Living 20

9. The Subterranean State 21

10. The Scorched Counsel 22

11. The Hollow Mourning 23

12. The Shepherd's Divide 24

13. Vapor and Void. 25

14. The Slip of Fate 26

15. The Bushel of Greed 27

16. The Essential Hook 28

17. The Hunger and the Habit. 29

19. Vesta and Vapor 31

20. Vows to the Morning. 32

21. The Paring of the Soul. 33

22. The Unguarded Sanctuary. 34

23. The Fertile Mirror. 35

24. The Silent Guides 36

25. The Duality of the Divide 37

26. The Stagnant Bloom................................. 38

27. The Season of the Fallen................................. 39

28. Flax in the Flame 40

29. The Seamless Bond 41

30. The Chiseled Stone 42

31. The Shadow of the Peak................................. 43

32. The Smoke of Preparation 44

33. The Void of Strategy 45

34. The Weight of the Blessing 46

35. The Paradox of the Sphere................................. 47

36. The Unshaken Crag................................. 48

37. The Image in the Clay................................. 49

38. The Steady Droplet 50

39. The Starving Palm 51

40. The Flood and the Clock 52

41. The Molting of Misery 53

42. The Greased Basin 54

43. The Widening Portal 55

44. The Empty Sanctuary 56

45. The Harvest of Insight 57

46. The Fluid Soul 58

47. The Wandering Stream 59

48. The Measure of Grace 60

49. The Cluttered Vault 61

50. The Auditory Mask 62

51. The Moving Stair... 63

52. The Exposed Bloom 64

53. The Burning Insight 65

54. The False Support... 66

55. The Morning Bloom 67

56. The Infinite Rind 68

57. The Ninety Crutches 69

58. The Ember and the Ash 70

59. The Dying Spark 71

60. The Morsel and the Mountain 72

62. The Tight Shoe of State 75

64. The Golden Strainer.. 77

65. The Waxen Stream 78

66. The Broken Bond 79

67. The Roasted Seed 80

68. The Common Grace... 81

69. The Twin Lights... 82

70. The Promise of Dawn 83

71. The Hollow Days 84

72. The Architecture of Silence 85

73. The Spindle's Orbit 86

74. The Ghost of Liberty 87

75. The Frayed Web 88

76. The Lost Harvest 89

77. The Scorched Crust 90

78. The Law of the Root 91

79. A Psalm for the Scattered 92

80. The Roasted Heart 93

81. The Corrosive Tongue 94

82. The Rotten Bed 95

83. The Hearth of Sacrifice 96

84. The Fire's Verdict 97

85. The Traitor's Smile 98

86. The Golden Cup 99

87. The Anatomy of a Jar 100

88. The Shadow in the Bed 101

89. The Law of the Flame 102

90. The Windshield of the Soul 103

91. The Unstoppable Sun 104

92. The Untied Knot 105

93. The Drunken Sentinel 106

94. The Archer of Time 107

95. The Burst and the Blaze 108

96. The Battery of the Being 109

97. The Stinging Truth 110

98. The Shield less Hearth 111

99. The Living Ghost 112

100. The Golden Lamp 114

101. The Honest Hearth 115

102. The Leak in the Dream 116

103. The Silent Bleeding 117

104. The Unfolding Joy 118

105. The Divine Verdict 119

106. The Watchman of the Soul 120

107. The Ten Witnesses 121

108. The Infinite Anchor 122

109. The Burden of Regret 123

110. Of Men and Storks 124

111. The Hundred-Legged Worm 125

112. In the Kingdom of Leaves 126

113. Lessons from the Dew 127

114. The Reed and the Fuel. 128

1 The Enduring Provision

When a father's discipline,
And a mother's counsel,
Rest within the heart and soul.
Upon the winding paths of life,
They serve as lasting sustenance—
Measured out, one grain at a time.

2 The Path of the Unwary

For him who does not stand alert,
Upon the road of insight,
Guided by his own clear thought.
The lure of the gambler's dice,
The intoxicant of an official's wine,
The poisoned jar of crooked gain.
For him who points a reckless finger,
Whose mind is whirled in a daze,
It will trip him and cast him down,
Like the bread of Passion.
A lethal, flowing current,
A jagged, stripped-bare wire.

3 An unanchored heart

A heap of flour without a shroud;
   To wander is to pass,
   To drift is to vanish—
Yielding to the vagrant wind.

4 **The Pebble and the Mote**

Of pebbles and of mote;
For those who tread upon me in scorn,
Who glimpse me through the slits of their lashes,
Or view me with the tail of a disdainful eye:
Grant me, O Lord, this prayer—
Become a pebble within their stride,
And a mote within their eyes.

5 Tether and Parchment

Of rope and parched meat;
Where did this ethos—
This thing called "Life"
Learn its craft?
The one strained to the limit,
The other withering away,
Searing in a hollow thirst.

6. The Softening Grace

When the skin of your life is brittle and gray,
And the world has beaten your spirit to stone—
Seek the oil that washes the sorrow away,
From the well of the Mercy that stands alone.
No debt is recorded, no payment is sought,
No paper is signed in the halls of the sky;
For the peace of the soul can never be bought,
By the gold of the earth or a mortal's lie.
He breaks the fetters, He shatters the shroud,
Raising the fallen from the embers and dust—
A voice of calm in the midst of the loud,
The only harbor for a heart of trust.

7. **No Smoke Without Fire.**

No smoke ascends where no fire burns
Upon the clay of the hearth;
No trumpet cries, no flute returns
A breath did not first unearth.
For not without a cause—
Nor without a reason's weight—
Does a hero yield his dying hope,
Or descend from the watchman's height
To vanish in the valley's slope.
....
Only when the bitterness takes hold,
Only when the home grows cold,
Does a father steal his heart –
Forsaking child, and wife,
And the humble shelter of his life.

8. The Toll of Living

A furnace of searing embers,
Void of ember or flame;
Blazing, parching,
Robbing the soul of rest,
Reducing a human being
To brittle bone;
Dragged forth by a chaos
Devoid of meaning—
The cost of living.

9. The Subterranean State

When strife, like a seedling,
Proliferates without a cure;
When love turns to ash,
And vitality begins to wane;
A nation, like a common root,
Seeks only the depths of the dust.

10. **The Scorched Counsel**

Wisdom is a priceless thing,
Not found in any merchant's bin—
But if the bells of trade should ring,
I'd bid you buy the light within;
To save the spirit from its sin.
To close the eyes against the sun,
To hear the word and not obey—
Is a race that's lost before it's run,
A debt that you must surely pay;
At the dawning of the day.
The price of silence is a fire,
The cost of ignorance is lead—
Lifting the pyre higher and higher,
Among the living and the dead;
Until the heavy words are said.
Love and fire are the same,
They melt the iron and the bone—
And he who speaks has felt the flame,
Beside the spirit's hollow throne;
To make the ancient secrets known.

II. The Hollow Mourning

23

When grief is staged as a melody,
And a groan is masked as a jest—
Beneath the gaze of the many;
Tears are stripped of their worth,
And the weeping soul is numbered;
Like the wild grass of the field,
Clutching a vanishing dew.

12. The Shepherd's Divide

One strikes with a sling's cold force,
Felling the flock like wind-blown grain;
He hunts them from the precipice—
From the high tower of his reign.
The other—**The True Guardian**—
Breathes life into the weary soul;
Charting a path through the valley of pain,
He shields the weak from their strife.
It is the spirit of the watcher,
The nature of the ruling order;
For the masses are ever the same—
Cast into the abyss by the tyrant,
Led to the pastures of grace by the Saint.

13. **Vapor and Void**

To this endless "hush,"
What rhythm can I lend?
A deep-rooted thorn,
An unyielding ghost of the past—
What herbal balm can mend?
The arrival I craved
Has withered in the waiting;
I have traded my pleas
For the silent defiance of youth.
...
The truth one dares not utter,
The hope one fails to grasp;
They are but shadows and fog—
Shifting form as the distance fades,
Dissolving into the void.

14. The Slip of Fate

We fancy ourselves masters,
Holding the world in a triumphant grip;
Yet not every bud that flowers,
Nor every harvest that matures,
Is meant for the reaper's hand.
If Time grants no favor,
And Providence offers no word;
The very bread for which we hungered,
The feast that wet the lips,
Shall crumble into the dust.

15. The Bushel of Greed

A generation that disdains
The weight of the future's hand;
An intellect has gone cold.
It defines its motherland
By the limits of its hunger—
A hollow measure bought and sold.
Every deed is meted out,
A calculated, stinted toll;
For the belly is the only scale
To weigh a nation's soul.

16. **The Essential Hook**

Love is the *Wheel* of our State
The shaft is severe,
The yoke is estranged;
The blade is discarded,
The lash is disengaged.
Scattered to the winds,
Fragmented and cold;
The master-link is broken,
And a million-fold power
Is left to grow old.
No land can prosper
By dragging the few, or hoisting the rest;
Cease the bitter push,
Put the malice to rest.
For if we think only as parts,
A nation apart;
The abyss is our cradle—
A shedding of leaves, in the dark.

17. The Hunger and the Habit

If you trade your soul for a crust of bread,
And break the seal of the ancient vow—
With hollow words that are better unsaid,
Upon a dark and heavy brow;
In the silence of the "now."
The path of the flesh is a lonely road,
Away from the culture, away from the light—
To carry a heavy and a bitter load,
Into the center of the night;
Away from every human sight.
For a habit is like a tethered rope,
That starts as a thread and ends as a chain—
Stealing the light and stealing the hope,
In the middle of the rain;
And the heavy, silent pain.
The more you wander, the more it binds,
Until the spirit is caught and still—
In the web that the weary spirit finds,
Against the sovereign, sacred will;

18. The Unlearned Judge

Exert your soul or hold your peace,
The outcome finds no sweet release;
For those who fail to tell apart
The noble grain from common weed,
The scholar's mind from hollow heart;
Will never lack a stone to throw,
Within their small and bitter row.

19. **Vesta and Vapor**

One dissolves in its own tears,
A searing light that steals its breath;
Bestowing vision, while courting death.
The other drifts in a silent plume,
Cloaking the world in a sweet perfume;
Merging its soul with the wandering air.
Such is the weave of the human loom—
The Candle's flare, and the Incense's bloom.

20. Vows to the Morning

Let my counsel be brief:

Do not cast aside the dew, nor your soul's well-being,

While the morning is yet new.

For sorrow ripens with the noon,

When you find they have fallen—

All too soon.

21. The Paring of the Soul

The Truth requires no raiment,
Naked and stark in the light;
While Lies and Love, like oil and mist,
Separate in the cool of the night.
Cover the wound as you may,
Running from what is true;
But like an onion beneath the blade—
A lie grows thin and reveals its hue.

22. The Unguarded Sanctuary

In the golden order of the hive,
Reserved for the sting and the sweet—
If a common ant begins to thrive,
The colony faces defeat.
Awaken, oh traveler!
For is it not the same?
If you willfully widen the fissure,
And offer the key to your union's frame—
To a stranger's prying pleasure.

23. The Fertile Mirror

To bear the burden, or to be the guest,
The path is yours, at your own behest.
Whether the fruit is charred or gold,
A flavor sharp, or a story told—
The choice was yours to hold.
For the soil and the silent mind,
Accept whatever they may find;
Wheat or tare, they make no plea—
They only grow what you set free.

24. The Silent Guides

In the realm of destiny,
Of sustenance and found grace—
No soul can ever discern
If they have found a permanent place.
Like a surging river
That claims the yielding land,
When a vision strikes the heart,
You ride the rushing tide—
Where the road and thought depart.
Providence and the Inner Thought,
The Master and the Unseen Track—
They carry you toward the far;
But they whisper not of the port,
Nor reveal the guiding star.

25. The Duality of the Divide

Behold the craft of the Divine!
A shroud of fog, a flash of light;
A jagged fall, a mountain's peak,
A hollowed gorge in sight.
The bridge we built with worldly wit,
To span the vast and shoreless blue,
Lies drowned beneath the rushing tide—
Lost within a provincial view.

26. The Stagnant Bloom

That emerald shade of yesteryear,
A memory of a former soul—
Has turned into a jagged spear.
Nurture it as you may,
With endless streams and tender hand;
But if the thirst for growth has fled,
And strength has turned to sand—
The seed that shuns the season's strife,
Ignoring heat and biting cold,
Can never claim the breath of life;
Its story is already told.

27. The Season of the Fallen

A canopy that flourished in the spring,
Yet withers when the winter winds sting—
Leaving the weary bird of the wild,
Unprotected, forsaken, and exiled.
Under the rule of the hollow and proud,
Where the cries of the hungry are loud—
Man is but a leaf on a dying bough,
Swept away by a ruthless plow,
In the darkness of a cruel vow.

28. **Flax in the Flame**

The timber burns to heat the round,
Of the griddle waiting for the grain—
While a heavy and a hollow sound,
Rises above the wind and rain;
In the middle of the pain.
Like flax that leaps when the clay is hot,
We jump and stir in the pan of fate—
Unwilling to accept our lot,
Within the dark and heavy gate;
Where the silent watchers wait.
The heat of the world is a fire bright,
Stealing the rest from the weary soul—
In the center of the lonely night,
Beyond the spirit's weak control;
To break the shattered vessel's bowl.
Our bellies are tight with a restless dread,
A movement born of the scorching air—
Searching for more than daily bread,
To answer the weight of a silent prayer;
And the heavy shadows everywhere.

29. **The Seamless Bond**

The legends of yore have passed into sleep,
With Tewodros's fire and Lalibela's stone;
The sweet, melting friendships we used to keep,
Have vanished like mist, leaving us prone.
Yet, we offer our praise!
For a bond like a zipper is forged in our day—
Its teeth interlocked, steady and true;
It yields not to pressure, nor gives us away,
But cloaks every secret from public view.

30. The Chiseled Stone

Had we but borrowed
The spider's wait, the ant's resolve,
The dove's calm heart, the bee's intent—
Our human burdens might dissolve.
We would not grind our years
Like a coarse and ancient wheel;
Ever chiseled, ever worn,
To a fate of cold and heavy steel.

31. The Shadow of the Peak

The height of Gheralta is a fearsome sight,
To those who watch it from the dusty plain—
Turning the golden day into a night,
Filled with the music of a ghostly rain;
And the heavy echo of a silent pain.
The road you haven't taken is a ghost,
Haunting the spirit with a hollow sound—
Until the things you fear the very most,
Are all the treasures that your heart has found;
Upon the holy and the sacred ground.
Life is a weaver of a silken chain,
It ties your courage with a thread of words
To make you suffer in a world of rain,
Where only cries of phantom grief are heard;
Like the weeping of a tethered, lonely bird.
You are driven like the herd toward the gate,
By fears of mountains that you never climbed—
Surrendering your spirit to a fate,
That is by shadows and by rumors timed;
In a world that's tattered and un-rhymed.

32. **The Smoke of Preparation**

The seeker kneels, the worker stands,
Both reaching for a hidden prize—
With weary hearts and steady hands,
Beneath the vast and silent skies;
Where the ancient wisdom lies.
They are the same, these two who wait,
With eyes fixed on the distant shore—
Standing before the golden gate,
Asking for a little more;
From the Master's endless store.
But the honey and the grace are kept,
For the one whose house is clean and bright—
While the shivering world has quietly slept,
Through the center of the night;
Waiting for the morning light.
An unwashed heart is a broken hive,
Where the spider spins a web of greed—
Where no holy thing can stay alive,
To answer every human need;
And water every bitter seed.
Burn the incense, offer the fast,
Scour the spirit with a sacred flame—
Until the shadows have quietly passed,
And you call upon the Holy Name;
Beyond the reach of fear and shame.

33. The Void of Strategy

The path is long, the feet are fast,
But the goal is nowhere found—
A phantom race that cannot last,
Upon the weary ground;
With a hollow, silent sound.
A storm of tongues, a clashing mind,
But the answer is not near—
Leaving the solution far behind,
In a world of doubt and fear;
Where the truth is never clear.
To sweat and strain with heavy breath,
But with no skill to guide the hand—
Is a slow and a lingering death,
Across the dry and weary land;
Where the ancient watchers stand.
"Vanity of Vanities!" the spirit cries,
When the heart is starved of light—
For unless the holy truth shall rise,
To end the long and heavy night;
There is nothing in our sight.

34. The Weight of the Blessing

Let them sharpen the thorn and the stone,
To scatter obstacles along your way—
But you are never truly alone,
In the heat of the long and heavy day;
Where the silent watchers stay.
If the blessing is poured from the height,
It becomes a garment that you wear—
A shield against the terrors of the night,
An answer to every silent prayer;
And the heavy shadows everywhere.
The prayers of the wicked are thin as dust,
Lighter than a gnat upon the breeze—
Corroded by the shadow and the rust,
Of the cold and the bitter seas;
That offers no moment of ease.
Do not fear the crocodile's weep,
Or the "mercy" of a hollow, lying tongue—
For the promises the heavens keep,
Are the songs that the ancient stars have sung;
Since the world was bright and young.

35. **The Paradox of the Sphere**

In one house, the clapping of hands,
In another, the tearing of hair—
Across the wide and the tattered lands,
A mixture of hope and despair;
Floating like smoke in the air.
The world is a prism of a thousand sides,
Reflecting the fire and the frost—
Where the shadow of sorrow quietly hides,
And the soul is won or is lost;
At such a heavy and bitter cost.
A gaming board for the cards of fate,
Where the infant and elder are thrown—
Beneath the vast and the silent gate,
Where the seeds of chance are sown;
And the harvest is never known.
It yields no mercy for the blade of grass,
Or the king on his golden throne—
Watching the seasons and centuries pass,
Like a heart made of hollow stone;
Leaving the spirit alone.

36. The Unshaken Crag

Let me be a stone of granite,
That the storm and flood cannot sway;
Standing firm on the edge of time,
Where the waters of truth find their way.
Perched upon the silent height,
Above the road where legends tread;
To see how the river and the years
Will weave the path that lies ahead.
For my people and my native dust,
To watch their fate—my only trust.

37. **The Image in the Clay**

49

When a nation breaks its sacred bond
With the spirit of the stream and the hallowed hill;
When it shatters its faith,
And its ancient, divine will—
It will feast upon its own children,
Dishonoring the **Eternal Potter**;
Who fashioned life from the humble earth,
And gave the clay a heavenly birth.

38. **The Steady Droplet**

We seek for joy in the thunder's roar,
In the lottery's luck and the wedding song;
Waiting for tents to grace our door,
Claiming that life has done us wrong.
But look behind the restless scene,
To the humble work and the daily pace;
It is the droplet, clear and clean,
That fills the vessel with lasting grace.
Happiness is a garden grown,
Saving the seeds that the moments sow;
By tiny drops, the truth is known—
That bit by bit, the wonders grow.

39. **The Starving Palm**

To one cursed with a craving eye,
Reveal not all where beauties lie.
From the subtle hues to the fiery red,
By the gin's fire and the honey-mead fed.
For surely you know, as the wise have said:
The **spoon** and the **palm** are never fed.
They cradle the feast, they guide the flow,
But remain as empty as the winds that blow

40. **The Flood and the Clock**

The passing rain is a fleeting thing,
Though it soaks the bone and chills the skin—
Wait for the song the birds will sing,
When the golden hours begin;
And the light comes rushing in.
I stretched the proverb like a string,
Across the bow of my weary mind—
Until I heard the secret ring,
Of the truth I was meant to find;
Leaving the shadows far behind.
Though the hardship tightens like a noose,
And the months are bitter, dark, and long—
The spirit must remain profuse,
With the echo of an ancient song;
To keep the shivering courage strong.
"Save yourself!" the wisdom cries,
When the torrent rises at the gate—
For under the vast and silent skies,
Nothing is fixed by a hollow fate;
If the heart is brave and great.
All shall pass like a river's flow,
Time and the flood move hand in hand—
Taking the high and taking the low,
Across the dry and weary land;
Where the ancient watchers stand.

41. **The Molting of Misery**

When the scales of toil are shed at last,
Like a serpent's skin upon the grass—
And you emerge from the winter's blast,
Watching the ghosts of your troubles pass;
Then come the voices, sweet and loud,
The praise of those who shunned the fray—
A thick and ever-lingering crowd,
Like shadows on a summer's day.

42. The Greased Basin

Time—the fleeting, ghost-like foe,
With no witness to its pace;
Who is man to stand and throw
A challenge to its silent face?
A basin slick with gilded grease,
Where every step is but a slide;
It shatters all your hard-won peace,
And cast your strength aside.
It breaks the frame and scars the hide,
With nowhere left to hide.
No feast is shared, no prize is claimed,
Until the Sun gives its decree;
For only when the Hours are tamed,
Can any soul be truly free.
Without the Day, no triumph stays—
Lost in the shifting maze.

43. The Widening Portal

Within a cell of velvet black,
When days are heavy and hearts are torn—
The soul that seeks the narrow crack,
Shall find the light of a distant morn.
Through a pinhole, truth shall seep,
A golden thread in a silver sea;
Stop gazing at where the shadows sleep,
And face the spark that sets you free.
Pry it open, bit by bit—
Bright,
And brighter yet!
Until the lamp of life is lit,
And the sun of truth has never set.

44. The Empty Sanctuary

A heart that knows no love,
A mind where shadows flee,
A hive that bears no sweetness—
Is a barren, hollow tree.
For void they shall remain,
And empty to the core;
Without the Creator's grace,
And the bees' golden store.

45. The Harvest of Insight

The toil of man is a river's flow,
A surging tide that comes and goes;
But keep your peace within its glow,
And reap the truth that wisdom shows.
For in the heart of understanding,
Where the frantic shadows flee—
You shall find the master-commanding,
The lock, the light, the living key.

46. **The Fluid Soul**

I offer you a "curse" of grace,
A blessing in a strange disguise:
Be like the water in its race,
Underneath the shifting skies.
Rise as vapor, light and free,
When the desert sun is bold;
Turn to stone, a silent sea,
When the winter's heart is cold.
Flow as wide as Tana's breast,
Through the valley and the glen—
For in the water's fluid quest,
Lies the victory of men.

47. The Wandering Stream

Like the Blue Nile, the Ethiopian soul
Has roamed across the distant shore;
But the dread of a late and weary return
Is a shadow that haunts the door.
For life in a stranger's land is harsh,
A vintage turned to vinegar and gall;
While the Awash, so wise and so still,
Found its grave within the mother's wall.

48. The Measure of Grace

More than the riches in a locked embrace,
Or the gems that sparkle on a kingly hand—
Is a heart that reflects the Creator's face,
The purest spirit in all the land.
For when a kind soul gives but a crumb,
With a finger moved by a love divine—
The cries of the poor shall at last grow dumb,
For in that small grain, the heavens shine.

49. The Cluttered Vault

An inbox filled with dross and gold,
The human mind, a restless crate;
Where ancient stories, new and old,
Are cast in heaps by love and hate.
Errors, truths, and fleeting news,
Are emptied in a single stream;
Blending all the darkened hues,
Within the fabric of a dream.
Yet, to clean this grimy well,
And wash away the debris of the years—
Is a labor where the ages dwell,
A task for silence and for tears.

50. The Auditory Mask

The breath of power is a plague,
A virus in the street—
A phantom wind, cold and vague,
That makes the nations retreat.
Why should you catch the frantic heat,
Or burn within their flame?
Why march to a distorted beat,
In a master's lethal game?
Against the words that poison deep,
A simple shield I ask—
Before you drift to endless sleep,
Put on your "Ear Mask."

51. The Moving Stair

I watched the horizon, craving the sun,
Counting the heartbeats until it was near;
But the distance was not in the race to be run—
It was only the weight of my hope and my fear.
The darkness may vanish, the light may appear,
To herald a day that is vibrant and new;
But time is a river that rings in your ear,
And the years will not pause for the glory in view.
Life is a carriage on a vertical track,
An elevator climbing through silence and gold;
There are no pausing and no turning back,
To grasp the beauty before we are old.

52. The Exposed Bloom

From the darkness of the hearth, he drew
The budding lips, the chest of pride;
Exposing all your worth to view,
Like malt within the sun to bide.
That photograph—it flew, it grew!
It had no lust, no hand to press,
No heart to burn with fleeting fire;
It gave us art, and nothing else,
A work beyond a man's desire.
How can I curse its cold caress?
Curse instead of the hands that weave,
Or those who massage in the gloom—
Who touches the strength we should believe,
Like pyramids in ancient rooms;
The ones who touch, and then they leave,
The fallen flower's silent doom.

53. The Burning Insight

To him who never felt the flame,
The fire is but a distant glow;
He gives the agony a name,
But does not feel the river's flow.
To him, hunger is a game.
A stranger's scar is but a line,
A story told in fading ink—
Until you make his burden thine,
And stand upon the jagged brink,
Where human souls at last entwine.
For wisdom is a stinging seed,
And truth is pepper in the eye;
It only answers in your need,
When hollow words and comforts die—
And wounds begin to ache and bleed.

54. The False Support

We taught the child to find his feet,
With songs of praise and gentle hand;
Encouraging the brave retreat,
From crawling on the dusty land.
But when his legs grew swift and strong,
To outruns those who led the race—
We tripped with the one we helped along,
To keep him in a lower place.
A hollow help, a cruel deceit,
To bind the soul and claim to free—
To drag the heart with leaden feet,
While singing songs of liberty.

55. The Morning Bloom

A person is a slender reed,
A fragile support in an hour of greed;
However tall they seem to stand,
They crumble in the reaper's hand.
The sun is set, the spirit's cry
Is lost beneath a leaden sky;
For joy is but a fleeting guest,
Before the silence and the rest.
More transient than the morning dew,
Our numbered days are small and few;
Before the grass can taste the rain,
The pulse is gone; the hope is slain.
A sunflower in the golden field,
To evening shadows, it must yield;
To bloom at dawn, to fade by eve—
Is all the legacy we leave.

56. **The Infinite Rind**

Wherever you stand on this restless earth,
From the moment of breath to the final sigh—
Sorrow has shared in the joy of your birth,
A faithful shadow beneath the sky.
A perfect fullness, a feast without end,
Is a phantom dream that the world cannot give;
For pain is a neighbor, a foe, and a friend,
In every city where mortals live.
Like the layers of onion, pungent and deep,
One trouble is shed as another appears;
A cycle of waking, a cycle of sleep,
A harvest of laughter, a harvest of tears.

57. The Ninety Crutches

Step by step, the ruin grows,
From the foot to the clouded mind;
A heavy debt, a liquid dose,
That leaves the upright soul behind.
Water for beer, and lies for the poor—
Neither can save what is rotten and sore.
A falling house, a swaying drunk,
Cannot be saved by the loudest cheer;
Though ninety crutches hold the trunk,
The end of the journey is drawing near.
For strength is a pillar within the breast—
Without it, the structure can find no rest.

58. The Ember and the Ash

A kiss is but a ritual dance,
A hollow rite of lip and breath;
A fleeting, fire-shadowed glance,
That leads the spirit toward its death—
The bitter fruit of a false romance.
Observe the smoker's cold intent:
He holds the flame against his soul,
Until the glowing light is spent,
And he has reached his selfish goal—
To leave the heart broken and bent.
He draws the smoke, he tastes the heat,
Then grinds the spark beneath his shoe;
Treading the beauty into the street,
As if the love were never true—
A victory turned to a cold retreat.

59. The Dying Spark

The flashlight's shell is but a ghost,
Without the stone that brings the light;
A hollow guard, a silent host,
Left shivering in the arms of night.
When the pulse was gone, the power flew,
The living frame is cold and dead.
When focus fails and the heart is torn,
The eyes are windows to an empty room;
Though a thousand sights are daily born,
They cannot dispel the inner gloom.
For vision is a spark of the soul's desire,
Without wisdom, there is no fire.

60. **The Morsel and the Mountain**

If you seek the path of light,
To bridge the hollow and the deep—
You must end the ancient night,
While the weary spirit's sleep;
And the promises you keep.
Striking down and taking all,
Will never lift the spirit high—
It only makes the courage small,
Beneath the vast and silent sky;
Where the heavy shadows lie.
Rise!
Rise above the clouds of greed,
Higher than the eagle's wing—
To answer every human need,
And hear the ancient spirits sing;
Before the crowning of the King.
It is easy to give from the overflow,
From the barn that's full of grain—
But if you truly wish to grow,
Beyond the reach of pride and pain;
In the middle of the rain.
Give the bread you meant to eat,
The very portion of your day—

To make the bitter journey sweet,
And wash the heavy grime away;
In a wild and wonderful way.

61. **The Gorge of Years**

The path is winding, deep, and wide,
Like the canyon floor where the river flows—
With nowhere for a soul to hide,
From the biting wind that always blows;
As the heavy shadow grows.
Man is the "Lonchina" on the steep,
Grinding its gears against the stone—
With promises that he has to keep,
In a world where he stands all alone;
Upon a cold and hollow throne.
Heavy with cargo, heavy with years,
It coughs and sputters in the heat—
Drying the sweat and the silent tears,
To make the bitter journey sweet;
In the middle of the crowded street.
This is the highway of our days,
A climb that tests the metal and the bone—
Lost within the dusty, silver haze,
Until the secret of the height is known;
And the harvest of the soul is grown.

62. **The Tight Shoe of State**

You watch the step and you watch the breath,
With a lingering and a jealous eye—
As if life were a debt to death,
Underneath the vast and silent sky;
Where the heavy shadows lie.
But even a toe within a boot,
That's tied too tight for a man to run—
Will strike against the very root,
Before the setting of the sun;
Until the heavy work is done.
The "Muffled Toe" begins to swell,
Against the leather and the lace—
A prisoner within a cell,
Searching for a wider space;
And the comfort of a face.
Go ahead, and cut the spirit down,
Before the wound begins to bleed—
For in every village and every town,
You plant the bitter, hollow seed;
To answer every hollow need.
The "Shadow" and the "Cadre" move,
With the same and sharp, relentless blade—
With nothing left for them to prove,
In the garden and the shade;
Where the ancient debt is paid.

63 The Uncarried Wealth

Leave the burden of hate behind,
And cast away the thorns of spite;
For a greedy hand and a bitter mind,
Must vanish in the coming night—
Where gold is stripped of all its light.
Neither your bread nor your silver pile,
Can cross the threshold of the dust;
They cannot buy a moment's smile,
Or save the heart from rot and rust—
When time demands its final trust.

64. **The Golden Strainer**

The furnace of your restless mind,
Has scorched the beauty of your brow;
Leaving the weary soul behind,
In the heat of a broken vow.
Will you turn to dust and ash,
In the shadow of a lightning flash?
Behold the sieve upon the floor,
A teacher of a quiet grace—
It drops the dust outside the door,
But keeps the treasure in its place.
It filters out the small and vain,
To save the substance and the grain.
To walk toward the morning light,
And leave the bitterness behind—
You must distinguish wrong from right,
Within the borders of the mind.
Be like the sieve, and learn to part
The heavy sorrow from the heart.

65. The Waxen Stream

As oil invades the paper's heart,
Spreading its stain with a ghost-like hand—
So does the winter of age depart,
To settle its frost upon the land.
We woke up to find, in the morning light,
The traces of a long and weary night.
For life is a current, narrow and deep,
Dripping from years like a melting light;
Into the valleys where shadows sleep,
Taking the fire, taking the sight.
The burning hope of a child's desire,
Is lost in the wax of the fading fire.

66. The Broken Bond

She lashed the spirit of the beast,
With cord and heavy rod—
Thinking that force would bring the feast,
Ignoring nature's God.
The cow has died, the milk is dry,
Beneath the heavy sod.
You seek the fruit of a captive soul,
With tethers tight and cold—
But power cannot play the role,
Of a love that is brave and bold.
Release the knot! For in the cage,
There is no luck or gold.

67. The Roasted Seed

He prays for rain on a barren plain,
While the grain for the sowing is burnt for a meal;
Feeding the hunger but losing the gain,
With a heart that refuses to see or to feel—
The rot that is turning the spokes of the wheel.
Can a herd multiply when the leader is slain?
Can life be born from a hollow desire?
The labor is wasted, the effort is vain,
Like seeking a fountain in the midst of a fire—
Or building a throne in the heart of the mire.
The earth shall open its wide, hungry jaws,
To swallow the dream and the kin of the fool;
For nature is bound by its unyielding laws,
And the breaker of truth is the breaker of rule—
Leaving a desert where once was a pool.

68. The Common Grace

Step by faithful step, the journey grows,
From a tiny spark to a blazing throne;
For he who trusts the Hand that all bestows,
Shall inherit worlds he has never known.
A crown of glory for a soul of trust,
Rising far above the world dust.
But if you cease to see the gift in breath,
Or find no wonder in the flowing spring—
Your spirit tastes a slow and silent death,
Where even the greatest joy can have no wing.
Though Heaven itself should fall into your lap,
Your unthankful heart is but a hollow trap.

69. **The Twin Lights**

In the service of the Just and True,
Where faith and labor intertwine—
The shadows flee the morning dew,
As stars of victory start to shine.
For when the barriers are gone,
And clouds of doubt are cast away—
The Inner Hope and Outer Dawn,
Conspire to light a perfect day.

70. The Promise of Dawn

The summer friends have taken flight,
The golden years have reached their end;
The morning fades into the night,
With neither hope nor any friend—
But darkness is a broken trend.
For though the shadows linger long,
The dawn shall find its way again;
To turn your weeping into song,
And wash away the bitter pain.
So, hold the bread and say your grace,
Before you win the coming race.

71. The Hollow Days

It is in the winter of a barren year,
That the soul perceives what the eyes ignore;
The mask of the world shall disappear,
To show the truths of the ancient lore—
The depth of love and the weight of fear.
There is a brier in the harvest grain,
A jagged rock on the silk of rest;
For joy is often the twin of pain,
A fleeting guest within the breast.
Be wise enough to expect the rain.

72. The Architecture of Silence

85

A beehive stands, a golden shell,
But silent is the honeycomb's cell;
For without the bees to fill the air,
The throne is stripped and the crown is bare—
A jar of clay in a desert's glare.
You build the towers toward the sky,
Where hollow winds begin to sigh;
But a city is not made of streets or walls,
Without the soul, the structures fall.
Can you taste the honey, sweet and clear,
When did the worker bees have fled in fear?

73. The Spindle's Orbit

The laws of Newton lose their grip,
When silver clinks within the hand;
The stars may fail, the sun may slip,
Across the stretches of the land—
But greed is king in every strand.
The moon obeys the earth's decree,
The tides respond to ancient light;
But there's a deeper gravity,
That rules the silence of the night—
The hunger for a golden sight.
From whirring spindles to the purse,
The human soul is tightly bound;
A spinning blessing, or a curse,
That keeps our feet on the ground.
In the math of gain and loss,
The spirit bears its heavy cross.

74. The Ghost of Liberty

The shackles and the heavy chain,
Are absent from her slender wing;
She flies above the dusty plain,
A proud and wild and hollow thing—
Who has no branch on which to sing.
They fell on the tree, they burned the glade,
They stripped the earth of every leaf;
And in the silence, they have made,
Her liberty is but a grief—
A transient and a bitter thief.
For freedom is a rooted grace,
A sanctuary, firm and deep;
But in this vast and empty space,
Where shadows of the forest sleep—
She has no self for her to keep.

75. **The Frayed Web**

88 (header)

A thousand reasons, a hundred please,
To hide the spark of a simple wrong—
But a broken loom can bring no ease,
And a tangled thread is never strong;
It trips the feet that have danced too long.
Beware the seed of a single lie,
For it holds a life you cannot tame—
It breeds in the dark of a shifting eye,
And multiplies in a house of shame;
Playing a wild and wicked game.
It grows like a cell in a secret tide,
Dividing itself into a frantic race—
With nowhere left for the truth to hide,
Within the lines of a weary face;
A wild amoeba in a holy space.

76. The Lost Harvest

89

We labored long when the earth was red,
With double yokes and a steady stride;
Preparing the path for the children's bread,
With the strength of youth and a father's pride—
But fortune has turned the rising tide.
The seed we saved for the coming spring,
The heart of the future, the soul of the field—
Took to the air on a sudden wing,
Refusing the life that the furrows yield;
Leaving the promise of plenty unsealed.
It fell on the rock, it fell on the flint,
Far from the reach of the nurturing clay;
A golden dream with a leaden tint,
Washed in the grief of a wasted day.
Oh, the corn of my land! How it withered away.

77. The Scorched Crust

The hope I wove in the loom of light,
Was torn away by a sudden gale;
Leaving me blind in the heart of night,
With a heavy heart and a broken sail—
A ghost within a silent veil.
My sanctuary felt the squeeze,
As the laughing voices filled the street—
I fell upon my weary knees,
Besides the ashes and the heat;
A bitter taste of a grand defeat.
The bread has burned, the crust is black,
But I will not fast when the sun is high—
I will not turn, I will not track,
A path where broken spirits lie;
I have no room for a hollow sigh.
I'll stand before the burning stone,
And speak to the heat of the iron grill—
Though I may stand here all alone,
I have the fire; I have the will;
The embers hear me, glowing still.

78. The Law of the Root

The weed arrives in sudden pride,
To carpet all the summer earth;
With nowhere left for truth to hide,
In a wild and hollow birth—
A life of little worth.
But age belongs to those who crawl,
Deep within the silent dust—
To build a base that will not fall,
Beneath the weight of time and rust;
A sanctuary of trust.
Behold the bamboo's secret toil,
The carrot's hidden, golden heart—
They find their glory in the soil,
Before they play their outward part;
A masterwork of art.

79. **A Psalm for the Scattered**

We have tasted the salt of our own weeping,
Our beds are drenched in the dew of pain—
While the rest of the world is quietly sleeping,
We shiver beneath a heavy rain;
And call Your holy name in vain.
We hold no claim to a righteous deed,
Our faith is a guttering candle-light—
But look at the ancient words we plead,
To lead us through the sudden night;
And restore our weary sight.
Let the iron gates be swung apart,
Let the shadows flee from the rising sun—
Mend the pieces of the shattered heart,
Before the race of life is run;
And the work of peace is done.
Halt the sword and stay in the hand,
That scatters the children to the wind—
Heal the wounds of the broken land,
Where the weary spirits have sinned;
And let the new life be pinned.

80. **The Roasted Heart**

The rawest bean and the unproven man,
Are silent in flavor and fame—
Following nature's mysterious plan,
Before they have walked through the flame;
Before they have earned them a name.
But stir them well in the heat of the fire,
Until the dark spirit awakes—
Rising above the smoke and the pyre,
In the path that a hero takes;
In the bond that destiny makes.
The sweetest aroma, the bravest of deeds,
Belong to the scorched and the brown—
For a soul that is tested is all that it needs,
To wear the high, heavenly crown;
And never to let the world down.

81. The Corrosive Tongue

94

Beware of the hunger of the hollow soul,
Who craves the smoke of a bitter lie—
Like a steady flame on a burning coal,
They will not let the silence die;
Until they've claimed the earth and sky.
They gather 'round with a rhythmic greed,
To taste the salt of a noble name—
Sowing the dark and the wordy seed,
To bring the highest spirit's shame;
And feed a wild and wordless flame.
Consider the **Amole**—the mountain's heart,
A jagged block of solid white—
How the ox's tongue, with a subtle art,
Can melt the stone in the dead of night;
And steal the morning's holy light.
The tongue is neither spike nor blade,
No glint of steel, no needle's sting—
But in the shadows, it has made,
It breaks the pride of every king;
And leaves the spirit a hollow thing.

82. The Rotten Bed

The hand that nurses and caresses,
Will rarely strike the faithful beast—
But habit wears its dark successes,
To turn the greatest to the least;
In a cold and bitter feast.
There is a law beyond the soul,
A habit seen as light and vain—
That slowly takes the full control,
And tighten every unseen chain;
Until the truth is slain.
Check your path and check your pace,
With the one who feeds and flouts—
For you have lost your inner grace,
In a world of shadows and of doubts;
Where the spirit's fire goes out.
You are like the thatch that's old and gray,
Rotting in the damp and cold—
Wasting all your light away,
In a story briefly told;
In a habit of heavy holding.

83. The Hearth of Sacrifice

It is a tale that's hard to tell,
A truth that rings within the ear—
Of how the brave are sent to hell,
To answer every hollow fear;
As the heavy shadows disappear.
The soldier is the pot of clay,
Set upon the jagged rock—
To burn the golden hours away,
And endure the heavy, iron shock;
While the silent watcher's mock.
The General is the silver spoon,
That tastes the fruit but avoids the fire—
Beneath the cold and white-faced moon,
Lifting the heavy curtain higher;
Above the funeral pyre.
The whistle screams, the fire grows,
Fed by the dry and brittle branch—
While only the broken vessel knows,
The weight of the sudden avalanche;
That no earthly power can staunch.
One is the master of the breath,
The other is the "Dreg-Taster" of the flame—
Walking the narrow road of death,
With no title and with no name;
In a world of pride and shame.

84. The Fire's Verdict

Fire and time, the ancient pair,
Boiling the egg and the root of earth—
One makes the liquid firm and fair,
The other gives to softness birth;
To prove the spirit's hidden worth.
The same struggle that breaks a man,
Will build another, stone by stone—
According to a secret plan,
That the suffering heart has known;
When standing in the world alone.
Distress is but a searing heat,
That tests the fiber of the soul—
To make the victory complete,
Or take a dark and heavy toll;
Upon the broken and the whole.

85. The Traitor's Smile

Behold the tooth that breaks the row,
To wound the mouth that kept it warm—
It does not care for the seeds we sow,
Nor the shelter from the winter storm;
In its wild and wicked form.
Think not that every open face,
Is a garden where the roses bloom—
For in that wide and hollow space,
There is a dark and a silent room;
A precursor to a sudden doom.
Like the hound that shows his yellow fang,
Before the leap and the final cry—
With a bitter and a metal twang,
Beneath a grey sky and a heavy sky;
Watching the honest moments die.

86. The Golden Cup

99

My hands are empty, parched, and dry,
And silence is the cooking fire—
But let my voice reach the sky,
Above the dust and the earthly mire;
To join the great and heavenly choir.
Fashion my mouth like a jar of clay,
To carry the water of your grace—
In the heat of noon and the fading day,
Within this lonely and weary place;
Before the shadow of your face.
Let no bitterness mar the taste,
No hunger steals the breath of prayer—
In the middle of the desert waste,
Beyond the reach of dark despair;
You are the breath; you are the air.

87. The Anatomy of a Jar

You speak of "necks" and "bellies" wide,
Like common jars of ancient clay—
But greatness is a world inside,
That does not fade or pass away;
On a fleeting and a dusty day.
The pitcher has a narrow throat,
The vessel has a belly's greed—
But they can neither sail nor float,
Nor plant a single, living seed;
In a moment of a human need.
Behold the man who lacks the "Head"—
The turning eye, the thoughtful grace—
He walks among the living dead,
With shadows on his empty face;
A ghost within a holy space.
For only he who looks behind,
And scans the road that lies ahead—
Can possess the sovereign mind,
And wake the spirit from the dead.

88. **The Shadow in the Bed**

Think not of enemies afar,
Who marches with banners in the sun—
But look beneath the evening star,
For where the silent webs are spun;
Before the battle had begun.
Consider the flea that haunts the sleep,
Wrapped in the darkness of the room—
Into the very soul it will creep,
To sow the seeds of sudden doom;
Within the sanctuary's gloom.
The greatest danger wears a smile,
And eat the salt from off your plate—
Practicing the ancient guile,
To turn a friendship into hate;
Besides the very city gate.
He kissed your cheek, he shared your light,
He knew the rhythm of your heart—
But in the middle of the night,
He played his cold and wicked part;
A master of a traitor's art.

89. The Law of the Flame

A wildfire rage and a young man's cry,
Are forces that no man can tame—
They reach to touch the leaden sky,
And give the world a darker name;
In a wild and a wicked game.
Without a mind to break the spark,
Without a voice to calm the roar—
The world is left within the dark,
To wash upon a bloody shore;
Where peace is seen no more.
For even the Ark, the holy stone,
Will perish in the mindless heat—
When wisdom's seat is left alone,
And chaos marches in the street;
To make the ruin complete.

90. The Windshield of the Soul

You left your heart upon the plain,
Bare and bleeding in the sun—
Expecting love, but finding pain,
Before the morning had begun;
And the hunter's race was run.
Your eyes were fixed upon the screen,
Scrolling through a hollow light—
While a thief, cunning and unseen,
Plucked your heart within the night;
And vanished from your weary sight.
Rest now, O soul, the damage is deep,
The organs of the spirit ache—
There are no promises left to keep,
After the final, heavy break;
For the sake of a digital mistake.
Like a windshield struck by a sudden stone,
The web of cracks will always stay—
You stand within the world alone,
Watching the fragments drift away;
At the end of a long and bitter day.

91. The Unstoppable Sun

Believe the word: The day will rise!
The "Gog and Magog" of the night—
Cannot conceal the morning skies,
Or steal the glory of the light;
From those who have the inner sight.
No hand can close the golden door,
No shadow bar your daily bread—
For peace will walk on the valley floor,
And raise the spirit from the dead;
Just as the ancient prophets said.
Behold the clouds, so young and fair,
The tender blossoms of the day—
Rising through the silver air,
To chase the leaden gloom away;
In a wild and radiant way.
The stars that boasted of their flame,
Within the absence of the sun—
Will hide their faces in their shame,
Before the day began;
When the victory of light is won.

92. **The Untied Knot**

Beware the one who seeks the knot,
But never means to share the bed—
Who leaves the spirit's holy spot,
And breaks the word that once was said;
To walk among the living dead.
They are the wind above the hill,
That carries nothing but the dust—
To work their wild and wicked will,
And satisfy a hollow lust;
In the ruins of a broken trust.
They sipped the soup from every hand,
To find a flavor fresh and new—
But cast your vessel on the sand,
And swore they had no taste for you;
Beneath a sky of leaden blue.
They turned your kitchen into a wreck,
And looked inside with vacant eyes—
To place a yoke around your neck,
And drape your soul in heavy lies;
Before the morning starts to rise.

93. The Drunken Sentinel

Politics and prayer, the coin and the cross,
Are pouring from a jar of bitter wine—
Where every gain is but a hollow loss,
Across the border and the holy line;
In a world of human and divine.
Behold the priest who's drunker than the guest,
Collapsed upon the porch of sacred stone—
Who gives the weary spirit little rest,
And builds a kingdom for himself alone;
Upon a cold and a hollow throne.
A nation filled with bellies large and vain,
Where greed is preached as if it were a grace—
Will harvest nothing but a sudden pain,
Within the lines of every weary face;
A ghost within a holy space.
They carry bags to gather in the toll,
In the name of God, they claim the silver's weight—
To buy the body and to break the soul,
Beside the temple and the city gate;
To seal a dark and a heavy fate.

94. The Archer of Time

Being there is not the deed,
Nor is the time the final word—
For every harvest needs a seed,
And every song a singing bird;
A voice that's clearly felt and heard.
The cards of life are dealt with to all,
Who watches the seasons drifting by—
But many trips and many fall,
Beneath a grey and silent sky;
Without a reason or a why.
It takes the eye, it takes the aim,
To hit the mark and win the prize—
To give the moment back its name,
Before the fading twilight dies;
In a world of riddles and of lies.
The man, the hour, the sacred place,
Must align in a perfect white—
To win the long and weary race,
And turn the darkness into light;
With a steady hand and a holy sight.

95. **The Burst and the Blaze**

You poked the hive with a jagged stick,
And filled the air with a choking haze—
Until the anger grew heavy and thick,
Turning the nights into golden blaze;
Across the count of the weary days.
You tread on the spirit like common mud,
Working the earth with a heavy boot—
Until the soil was stained with blood,
Reaching down to the ancient root;
Where the seeds of silence remain mute.
A tire can only hold so much,
Before it shatters the iron rim—
And feels the fire's scorching touch,
When the light of mercy begins to dim;
At the singing of the funeral hymn.
There is a measure to every grief,
A boundary to the longest chain—
The reign of the shadow is cold and brief,
Beneath the weight of the silver rain;
And the heavy echo of the pain.

96. The Battery of the Being

Between the "Her" and the "Him,"
Between the "Now" and the "Then"
When the golden light begins to dim,
In the world of weary men;
Beyond the reach of every pen.
The difference is a burning will,
A hunger to arise and run—
To climb the steep and jagged hill,
Before the setting of the sun;
Until the heavy work is done.
You are a vessel of a hidden power,
Like a battery's silent, potent cell—
Waiting for the darkest hour,
To break the heavy, iron spell;
And escape the spirit's hollow well.
But if those inner current fails,
And the chemistry of hope is lost—
The spirit lowers all its sails,
To pay the heavy, bitter cost;
Beneath the biting and the frost.
Your grave is dug, your shroud is wet,
The moment that your passion dies—
The sun of destiny has set,
Beneath the vast and silent skies;
Where the heavy shadow lies.

97. The Stinging Truth

Life is like the onion's core,
Wrapped in coats of bitter brown—
Standing at the spirit's door,
To cast the shivering courage down;
Within the center of the town.
You cannot peel the grief away,
In a single hour of the night—
You must confront the golden day,
And wait for the coming of the light;
To set the heavy burden right.
How can one dance the "Eskista" beat,
When the eyes are flooded by the rain?
Walking through the crowded street,
With the echo of a silent pain;
Upon the spirit's holy plain.
Hardship has a rugged skin,
Tougher than the iron bar—
Searching for the light within,
Beyond the reach of every star;
To tell us who we truly are.

98. The Shield less Hearth

Without the trees to break the gale,
The grass-roofed hut is left to mourn—
Behind a thin and a tattered veil,
Where the spirit is weary and torn;
By the winds that are newly born.
A house without a guardian tree,
Is a harbor without a shore—
Where the storms can wander wild and free,
To trample through the open door;
And haunt the valley floor.
They cut my shadow in the light,
Long before the branches grew—
To leave me naked in the night,
Beneath a sky of leaden blue;
Where the coldest currents flew.
Now every wind that passes by,
Steps upon my sacred ground—
Beneath a grey and a silent sky,
Where the echoes are the only sound;
And no shelter can be found.

99. The Living Ghost

Tremble for the soul you claim to hold,
If the fire in a brother's room—
Is to you a story that is told,
Without the shadow of a coming doom;
In the silence of the hollow tomb.
If a life is taken in the street,
And it seems no more than a fallen hound—
While you walk with cold and steady feet,
Upon the holy and the weary ground;
Where the secrets of the heart are found.
If the scream for mercy is a "task,"
Something to be noted and ignored—
Then take away the silver mask,
And put away the hollow, rusted sword;
Before the judgment of the Lord.
You are the one who truly died,
Lethal and cold in your apathy—
With nowhere left for the "Man" to hide,
In the desert of your vanity;
And the ruin of your sanity.
Better the grave for the one who fell,
Than the frozen heart within your frame—
For you are living in a silent hell,
Without a title and without a name;

In a world of pride and shame.
Fear your "humanity."
When one house burns,
and to you it seems
like a forest hut—
When another house is destroyed,
and to you it seems
like a puppy's kennel—
When the cries for life
appear to you as mere noise,
Do not dare to say,
"I am human!"
For beyond those who suffer,
it is you who has already died.
Fear your "humanity."

100. **The Golden Lamp**

There is a sweetness in the mind,
That honey never could provide—
A treasure that the seekers find,
With the spirit as a faithful guide;
Where the ancient words reside.
Your counsel is the morning sun,
Upon a path of jagged stone—
Before the race of life is run,
I walk no more within the lone;
With a light that I have known.
Accept my praise, O Source of Light,
For every truth that made me whole—
For leading me through every night,
And mending the fragments of my soul;
Toward a high and sacred goal.

101. The Honest Hearth

If the cupboard is empty of grain,
And the vessel is dry to the bone—
Do not seek a harvest of pain,
To offer a seed you have sown;
In a field that was never your own.
The bread that is baked in a sin,
Will turn into ash in the mouth—
No matter how golden the skin,
Or how far it travels to south;
To settle the spirit of drought.
The wine of oppression is sour,
Though it flows from a silver tipped jar—
It wilts every beautiful flower,
And leaves a permanent scar;
Beneath the morning star.

102. **The Leak in the Dream**

I was filled like a jar at the height of the feast,
By the words of the wise and the songs of the sane—
Until the red sun settled down in the east,
And the dream came to scatter the golden grain;
Beneath a cold and a phantom rain.
Tell me, O Dream, why you battle the light?
Why must you challenge the peace of the day?
To hollow the spirit within the long night,
And carry the fruits of my labor away;
In a dark and a desperate disarray.
There is a sinkhole beneath the mind's feet,
A hole in the middle where reality bleeds—
Where the day and the darkness awkwardly meet,
To bury the flowers and water the weeds;
And hollow the strength of my greatest deeds.

103. **The Silent Bleeding**

Every time the cactus leans,
Against the thorn tree's bitter edge—
It loses all its inner greens,
Upon the mountain's jagged ledge;
A victim of a broken pledge.
The thorn tree does not feel the sting,
Or value every drop of dew—
It only knows the pain it brings,
To everything it ever knew;
Between the many and the few.
The sinner walks a path of grace,
While justice strikes the guiltless head—
A shadow falls across the face,
Of those who offered only bread;
Within the silence of the dead.
For tears are fire in the end,
To burn the hands of those who slay—
Protect the spirit of the friend,
And wash the heavy grime away;
At the dawning of the day.

104. The Unfolding Joy

Do not seek a knot of gold,
Or a number in a ledger's line—
For joy is not a story told,
But a secret and a deep design;
That makes the inner spirit shine.
It is the work you do with pride,
It is the love that starts to bloom—
The rising of a gentle tide,
That scatters every trace of gloom;
And fills the spirit's quiet room.
Happiness is a living thing,
A seed that's planted in the clay—
The melody that spirits sing,
Throughout the labor of the day;
In a wild and wonderful way.
Conceived in hope and born in light,
It grows as every effort heals—
To lead the soul through every night,
And reveal what the heart reveals;
As the heavy wheel of seasons.

105. The Divine Verdict

The blade is snapped, the gun is stilled,
By a hand that moves from high above—
When the cup of ancient grief is filled,
Beyond the reach of human love;
Beneath the shadow of the dove.
Gather your horses, bring your men,
Let the generals shout their empty pride—
But what was written with the pen,
Has nowhere left for kings to hide;
Against the turning of the tide.
The days are numbered, one by one,
The weight of sin is clearly shown—
Before the setting of the sun,
The seeds of justice have been sown;
Upon a cold and hollow throne.
"Mene, Tekel" is the word,
Written in the spirit's flame—
A voice that finally must be heard,
To put the arrogance to shame;
And strip the glory from the name.

106. **The Watchman of the Soul**

He who fashioned every heart,
And knows the rhythm of the breath—
Who sees the ending from the start,
And holds the keys of life and death;
Beneath the vapor's rising wreath.
His gaze descends like morning dew,
To find the ones He calls His own—
With a vision sharp and new,
From the heights of a sacred throne;
Where the seeds of grace are sown.
Happy is the man whose sin is veiled,
Whose faults are buried in the deep—
When all the human efforts failed,
There is a promise He will keep;
While the tired world is fast asleep.
With a spirit clean and an honest word,
He walks the path the righteous know—
A silent prayer that's always heard,
Where the waters of the spirit flow;
In a soft and a holy glow.

107. The Ten Witnesses

Why do you think He watches long,
When do you lift your arms in prayer?
To hear the rhythm of your song,
Or see the burdens that you bear?
No—He looks for justice there.
Ten digits measured by His will,
To hold the weight of every Law—
To keep the restless spirit still,
And mend the ancient, human flaw;
With a deep and holy awe.
You spread your fingers, one by one,
And swear your heart is clean and light—
But before the setting of the sun,
And the coming of the night;
The hands reveal the hidden fight.
The price of hands is only known,
When you reach to take the sacred prize—
By the seeds that you have sown,
Beneath the vast and silent skies;
Before the King of perfect eyes.

108. The Infinite Anchor

Truth is the first and final sound,
The seed from which the heavens grow—
The holy and the sacred ground,
Where all the living waters flow;
And the ancient spirits go.
It is the light upon my path,
A crown of glory for the soul—
To shield me from the winter's wrath,
And make the broken fragments whole;
Under Your sovereign control.
If this word should ever fade,
And leave me in the bitter cold—
Within the silence and the shade,
With nothing for the heart to hold;
Like a story never told.
I cannot think, I cannot see,
A world without Your holy breath—
For what would then become of me,
In the shivering realm of life and death;
As the spirit wandereth?

109. The Burden of Regret

The very mud you trample today,
Beneath your feet at the threshold;
Will become the burden you bear tomorrow,
Rising to weigh upon your shoulders.
Death and the pain of parting,
Are the destiny of every soul;
A universal lot we share,
A cycle from which none can hide.
To care and to aid while life remains—
This is where the meaning lies.
For what comfort is a beaten chest,
To the one who lies in silence?
Like the goats descending from Gilead,
Downward toward the dark abyss;
We watched him sink into the void,
Yielding him to the grip of death.
For while he lingered on his bed,
We were hollowed out by greed;
And our malice was a heavy stone.

110. Of Men and Storks

When the nest turns cold and grey,
When delight has ebbed away,
Their destiny is bound as one—
The wandering man and the stork.
He bolts the door and turns away,
Leaving the hollow house behind.

III. The Hundred-Legged Worm

Though he has fifty feet,
Or even a hundred,
This humble worm;
He cannot scale a hundred trees,
By grasping them all at once.
So, gather your wisdom!
Select just one,
And hold fast to that single branch.

112. In the Kingdom of Leaves

To captivate the wandering eye,
It is the vibrancy of youth,
This cloak of emerald, green.
Yet, what is its fleeting worth?
For yellow is no symbol of hope,
Within the kingdom of leaves;
It is but a sign of the descent,
Of withering before the bloom.
Famine and the biting frost,
War and the crushing hail;
The leaf and the generation—
A haunting parallel,
A strange and striking bond.

113. **Lessons from the Dew**

If I share what the dew has taught me, heed my words:
In the budding of hope,
Within that which withers hope;
In the kindling of light,
Within that which snuffs out the flame;
In the severing of the wire,
Even as it binds the connection;
Serving as a humble needle,
While forcing the plow to be dropped;
Choosing the finest seed,
While stripping it from its lineage;
Let not your heart be consumed by fire.
The dew that clings,
To every blade of grass and leaf;
It has no fate but to fall,
It cannot endure the midday sun;
It vanishes as if it were nothing.
Only you, stay patient;
Do not let your sorrow overflow.

114. **The Reed and the Fuel.**

Knowledge and skill combined;
The whittled reed, the caster seed-
Intertwined to form a light.
Wrestling through the dark of night,
To secure the evening meal.

Thank you for reading these poems . Hopefully, you enjoyed it.

To share with friends:

From: --------------------------------

To: -----------------------------------

ZeGeray Desta
2026 (2018 E.C)

www.ingramcontent.com/pod-product-compliance
Lightning Source LLC
Chambersburg PA
CBHW071339150726
47997CB00002B/798